Ben Carson & Hillary Clinton:
Likeable or Unlikeable Presidential Candidates

Michael Joshua

ISBN: 1519109504
ISBN-13: 978-1519109507

DEDICATION

This book is dedicated to all those interested in the political candidates running for the US Presidency in 2016.

CONTENTS

Michael Joshua

ACKNOWLEDGMENTS

At the time this book was written, Ben Carson and Hillary Clinton, among others, were running for Presidential candidacy for the 2016 elections. I wrote this book to present both Ben Carson and Hillary Clinton's sides on all the main topic issues, just in case you have not been following the debates or can't keep track of them all. My hopes is that this book will provide you with the views of both these candidates in one place so it's easy to compare and contrast them.

CHAPTER 1: INTRODUCTION

This book is meant as a guide to the agenda of the two major players in the 2016 US presidential race. Although at the time this book was written, it is still unsure who the Presidential candidates will be, Hillary Clinton of the DNC and Benjamin Carson of the GOP are vying for their respective party's nomination for presidential candidacy.

It is important for the people to learn where these two presidential hopefuls stand on major issues. Knowing their stance and background will help the reader develop an idea of how each candidate might perform if elected to office.

It is not just necessary to understand the stance, the reasons behind this positon should also be explored. This book fills the requirement of providing the background knowledge that will help you see beyond the political buzzwords and grasp the true picture behind the carefully orchestrated media campaigns of the candidates. Get a glimpse of their agenda and make the responsible decision when it comes to voting.

CHAPTER 2: THE US PRESIDENTIAL ELECTION 2016

Americans head for polls once again in 2016 and will vote in the 58th presidential election. The current President, Barack Obama completes his second term in office and since the constitution prohibits from running for a third term, the major political parties, the Democrats and the Republicans must choose a new nominee that will contest the national elections, representing their respective sides.

The primaries and caucuses will start from February 2016 and go on till June 2016, in this process voters choose a slate of delegates, these will ascend to a political party's nominating convention. The nominee for the presidential race from a party is chose by these delegates.

CHAPTER 3: REPUBLICANS (GOP) VS DEMOCRATS (DNC)

The current list* of candidates who are trying to get the nomination of the Republican Party are:

- Donald Trump (24.3)
- Ben Carson (23.3)
- Marco Rubio (12.3)
- Jeb Bush (5.3)
- Rand Paul (3.7)
- John Kasich (3.7)
- Carly Fiorina (3.0)
- Mike Huckabee (2.7)
- Chris Christie (2.3)
- Rick Santorum (0.7)
- George Pataki (0.3)

The candidates* for the Democrat nomination are:

- Hillary Clinton (56.5)
- Bernie Sanders (33)
- Martin O'Malley (3)

These are the major ones, others (might have withdrawn their bids) include: Joe Biden, Lincoln Chafee, Lawrence Lessig, and Jim Webb.

*The lists are ordered according to the popularity percentage of the candidates as per the time this book was written.

CHAPTER 4: THE REPUBLICAN: BEN CARSON

Benjamin Carson, best known in the field of neurosurgery, has made his foray into the world of politics. He moves away from one high-stake and high-impact arena field to enter an arena even more pressure filled and exacting.

He is someone who is used to having lives depend on him in his medical work, and he has held up to that enormous pressure with great success. It is very interesting to see how he would deal with the pressures of being president of the most powerful nation in the world.

He has proved to be a major contender and has surged ahead in the polls, currently trailing the GOP front-runner, Donald Trump. His kindly voice and comforting demeanor puts people at ease. He has a few controversial stances and some predictably traditional ones; we take a look at the issues in details.

Early Life and Family

Ben Carson is a 64 year old neurosurgeon (now retired), born in Detroit, Michigan. On the 18th of September 1951. He grew up in a single-parent home, his mother raised him and his older brother by herself. Carson's mother had to often work two to three jobs at once, the family was poor and relied on government assistance.

Carson describes his early life in his book, Gifted Hands, he paints the years of his childhood and youth as being spent in a haze of violence and anger. He says that he had trouble controlling his temper and would lash out at people.

A specific incident is described in his book, involving a violent outburst, during which he tried to stab his school friend with a knife, fortunately the knife hit the friend's belt buckle and no one got hurt.

This incident affected Carson so much that he decided to change his ways, he looked towards the Bible for guidance, the teachings had a transformative effect on him and he claims that he conquered his temper after that once and for all.

Education Background

Ben Carson is a graduate of Yale University and studied medicine at the University Of Michigan Medical School. He attended Southwestern High School in Southwest Detroit. In high school he participated in the Us Army program, Junior Reserve Officer Training Corps (JROTC) and rose to the rank of cadet colonel.

Medical Career

Carson finished medical school and went on to complete a residency at the Johns Hopkins Hospital. He moved to Australia when he accepted a position at t Sir Charles Gairdner Hospital located in Perth. He later on rejoined John Hopkins in the senior capacity of Director of Pediatric Neurosurgery. His specializations in surgery included: traumatic brain injuries, epilepsy, spinal cord tumors, brain tumors, neurological and congenital disorders, etc.[1]

A major breakthrough he made involved developing a surgical technique that involves removing a part or all of a brain in order to control a severe seizure disorders that occur in children.

He also led a team of neurosurgeon that helped separate a set of conjoined twins, who were joined at the back of the head. The twins were seven months old when this procedure was performed. Carson went on to perform an additional four separation surgeries.

Publications and Media

Ben Carson has authored eight books over his career and even had a movie made that is based on his life story. Apart from the medical publications he is the author of the following books:

1. What I Believe a Collection of My Syndicated Columns (2015)

2. One Vote Make Your Voice Heard (2014)
3. Take the Risk Learning to Identify Choose and Live with Acceptable Risk (2007)
4. Managing in the Middle (2006)
5. The Big Picture Getting Perspective on What's Really Important in Life (2000)
6. The Big Picture (1999)
7. Think Big Unleashing Your Potential for Excellence (1996)
8. Gifted Hands the Ben Carson Story (1996)
9. Ben Carson (1992)
10. Think Big (1992)
11. Gifted Hands (1990)

Public Opinion

Carson is enjoying a relatively high position when it comes to polls, currently he stands at the second position behind the GOP front-runner, Donald Trump. During mid-November, Carson was polling at 23%, this is about 21% above the score of the average GOP candidate. The poll numbers have been trending upwards since November.

Potential Challenges Faced by Ben Carson

The one thing that will definitely prove to be an issue is that Ben Carson does not have any political experience, he has never held elected office. His first major foray into the world of politics is a bid for the most highly contested office in the world. So far he seems to have proved capable of handling the press and the pressures.

Whether things go well for him or not, whether he gets the GOP candidacy or not, the pressure will increase in any case once the campaign gets serious, it would be interesting to see if this doctor, who performed brilliantly in the high-pressure environment of complicated neurosurgery, manages to do the same in the complex world of high politics.

Major Scandals and Controversial Viewpoints

The biographical narrative provided by Ben Carson has been challenged by major news outlets such as CNN. The investigations by media outlets allege that the documented facts do not support Carson's story, these have been rubbished by Carson as a "witch hunt"[2] by the media.

The following incidences of his past are being questioned:

1. CNN interviewed nine of his classmates and neighbors, neither of them categorize Carson as violent, this led to the media questioning the accuracy of the stabbing incident, since the friend he allegedly tried to stab has remained anonymous so far.[3]
2. Carson claims that he helped protect white students when a race riot broke out in his high school in response to the killing of Martin Luther King Junior. The interviews by Wall Street Journal could not find anyone who could corroborate this story.[4]
3. Carson claims that he was offered a scholarship to West Point, but the academy has no record of Carson ever trying to seek admission, West Point does not offer scholarships at all. [5,6]
4. Carson had a connection with a questionable pharmaceutical company, Mannatech, he had given speeches at several events of Mannatech. Carson denies that he had any significant connections with the company that has had a troubling legal record.

Ben Carson has also been criticized for some controversial statements and viewpoints, some of the noteworthy ones are:[7]

Carson stated in a 1998 commencement speech that the Pyramids of Giza did not serve as tombs for ancient Egyptian Pharaohs, instead they were large grain structures meant for storing grain and were built by Joseph, the son of Jacob (as described in the Bible). Archeological experts disagree with his statements.

Carson rejects the theory of evolution and also considers carbon dating to be invalid because these notions go against the Christian belief.

Carson has also made remarks about homosexuality that angered a lot of gay rights activists, he later apologized for his comments.

Historians were upset when Carson expressed his thoughts on the Holocaust, he said that the enormous tragedy could have been averted if Jewish people had access to guns. This view is widely contested by historians and critics.

Presidential Elections 2016 and the Campaign

Ben Carson was an independent before the presidential bid, he officially joined the Republican Party on the 4th of November 2014. He officially launched his bid for the Republican presidential nomination in Detroit on 4th of May 2015.

Carson has raised an impressive $20.8 million in campaign funds during the third quarter, this figure is the highest of any Republican candidate. The spending rate, termed the burn rate is at 69%. This is high, usually candidates prefer to save and invest in the later times of the campaigning.

CHAPTER 5: THE DEMOCRAT: HILLARY CLINTON

Hillary Clinton is the former Secretary of State of the US, no stranger to politics, Mrs. Clinton is currently the front runner for the Democratic nomination. This is her second bid for the Presidency, she has previously campaigned in the Democratic primaries in 2008.

She served as the 67th United States Secretary of State under the current President Barack Obama. She has had a long political career and proved in the beginning of her law career to be a bright and highly capable woman.

Early Life and Family

Clinton is a native of Chicago, born Hillary Diane Rodham on 26th of October 1947, she comes from a United Methodist family. She was raised by her parents in a suburbs of Illinois with her two brothers.

The family was politically conservative and not very active in politics but Clinton was involved in campaigns as a volunteer since a very young age, she canvassed Chicago's South Side during the 1960 US elections when she was thirteen. Clinton's political views were largely shaped by her high school history teacher and her Methodist youth minister.

She married former US President Bill Clinton in 1975, they have one child, a daughter named Chelsea.

Educational Background and Law Career [8]

Clinton attended Wellesley College as a political science major and then went on to graduate from Yale Law School. During the postgraduate studies she also worked as a staff attorney for the Children's Defense Fund and was also a consultant for the Carnegie Council on children.

She was also on the impeachment inquiry staff which was responsible for advising the House Committee on the Judiciary during the troublesome time of the Watergate scandal.

Role as the First Lady [9]

Bill Clinton was elected the president in 1993, Hillary Rodham Clinton therefore became the First Lady of the US. Her distinguished professional career and postgraduate degree made her unique amongst the First Ladies of the past.

She was responsible for vetting top level appointees to the Clinton administration. She played an active role during her husband's presidential campaign and during the presidency.

During this period she also chaired a Task Force which created a national healthcare reform plan. She played a major role in the passage of the State Children's Health Insurance Program. She travelled widely and played a role in US diplomacy.

Political Career

The highest office held by Hillary Clinton in the long political career is Secretary of State (2009-2013) before that she was a member of the Senate (2001–2009). Before that she served as the first lady during her husband, Bill Clinton's presidency from 1993-2001.

She also ran for the presidency in before but later conceded the Democratic nomination to Barack Obama when it became clear that Obama held the most delegate votes.

She later served in Obama's cabinet as Secretary of State. She has served as an elected official for a period of eight years.

Publications

Clinton has authored numerous news articles as well as scholarly articles throughout her career. During her years as the First Lady of the United States, from 1995 to 2000, Clinton also wrote a weekly syndicated newspaper column titled "Talking It Over".

She wrote the following books that provide a detailed glimpse into her political views and her life.

1. It Takes a Village: And Other Lessons Children Teach Us (1996)

2. Dear Socks, Dear Buddy: Kids' Letters to the First Pets (1998)
3. An Invitation to the White House: At Home with History (2000)
4. Living History (2003)
5. Hard Choices (2014)

Living History is a detailed autobiography and Hard Choices is a second memoir and the most recent publication.

Public Opinion

Currently the Democratic favorite and front runner, Clinton is polling in at a high 54%, this is an impressive position, which places her 45% above the average Democrat candidacy-hopeful in the field.

Potential Challenges She Faces

Foreign Policy:

The fact that she has served in the Obama cabinet as the Secretary of State lends her a significant advantage over other presidential candidates when it comes to matter of foreign policy.

However, this may prove to be double-edged sword, the mistakes of the past administration might bring about more issues, the major challenges that will trouble Clinton are:

The response of the Obama administration to the rampant rise and widespread activities of the terrorist group, ISIS has not been adequate or effective.

The question of how to respond to the situation in Syria will also be an important one. Clinton has advocated that America needs to play a more active and muscular role when it comes to handling threats as serious and dynamic as ISIS.

Judging from the statements that she has made during the campaign, Clinton apparently seems to plan a tougher approach to these issues than the Obama administration.

Presidential Elections 2016 and the Campaign

Clinton announced her intention to run for President during April 2015 and formally launched her campaign. No stranger to political campaigns, she has been on a highly organized and systematic track for the past 31 weeks.

The total funds raised for the campaign amount to $101 million, this amount is the second highest raised by any Democratic candidate. The major Super PACs include American Bridge; Correct the Record and Priorities USA.

The official campaign committee is called Hillary for America. The campaign is spending the raised funds at a whopping 86% burn rate, major expenses incurred includes, media buys, payroll and online advertisements.

CHAPTER 6: A CLOSER LOOK AT THE ISSUES

The issues have been broken down into five broad categories of major US concerns:

1. Domestic Concerns
2. Economic Issues
3. Social Issues
4. Entitlements
5. National Security and Foreign Policy

The major domestic concerns include issues related to:

Gun Rights, Gun Crimes, Criminal Sentencing, Death Penalty, War on Drugs, Marijuana Legalization, Transportation Infrastructure, Hurricane Recovery, Environmental Protections, Nuclear Power, Net Neutrality, Internet Freedom, Government Secrecy, Open Government and Voter Registration

Issues of Import Regarding Economy:

Corporate Regulation, Corporate Welfare, Recession Bailout, Mortgage Crisis, Budget Deficit, Environment vs. Economy, Oil Drilling, Climate Change, Renewable Energy, Government Privatization, Campaign Finance Reform, Capital Gains Tax, Inheritance Tax, and Tax Reform

Social issues include:

Abortion, Family Planning, Stem Cells, Gay Rights, Defense of Marriage Act, Families and Children, Foster Care Service, School Prayer, Flag Issues, Personal Faith, Values and Principles, Gambling and Casinos and Partisanship.

Entitlement concerns include issues such as:

Medicare/Medicaid, Union Policy, Employment Policy, College Policy, Schools, Education Reforms, Welfare etc.

The national security hot points being discussed by the candidates include:

Terrorism policy, reaction to terrorist groups, Syria, Defense spending, America's role in foreign conflicts, a few issues of the past such as the Iraq war, 9/11, and the Afghan War.

Every presidential candidate makes his or her stance very clear on these issues and offer their unique take on the solutions that they will implement in elected to office.

These issues highlight the concerns of the typical American. How the candidates plan to tackle these problems and opportunities determines what kind of leader they will be.

These issues are broad and complex, no one expects the presidential candidates to have in-depth knowledge about each of these, but the American public demands that the leader be passionate about solving these issues.

The common people mostly decide their vote based on how the domestic concerns will play out. The candidates cannot only focus on domestic issues, their entire approach must be planned if they wish to convince the American public of their viability as presidential candidates.

The most important of these concerns and the stance that Clinton and Carson take on these is described in detail in the following chapters.

CHAPTER 7: BEN CARSON'S STANCE ON MAJOR ISSUES

1. Domestic

Gun Rights

Carson is an avid supporter of the 2nd Amendment, he holds the opinion that no one should tamper with this important piece of legislation. These are some of his major views on this issue:

- Weapon registration should not be mandatory, law-abiding citizens should have the rights to own guns without having to register them.
- Registering guns means the government can take them away if they want to
- Believes that the use of semi-automatic weaponry in the cities is a bad idea but is acceptable in rural settings.

Gun Crimes

He believes that horrific incidents such as school shootings and hostage situations can be controlled if the people in authority have better training and have access to weapons that they can use in case of an attack. Commenting on the incident at Umpqua Community College, he said that the proper way to react when such a horrific incident occurs is to refuse to be a victim and take control of the situation. These comments were not favorably received and were seen as advocating victim-blaming. He has stated the following views [10] when it comes to gun crimes:

- Effects of gun violence are less devastating than losing the Second Amendment rights.
- He suggests that the violence incidence can somehow be controlled or minimized if the victims took appropriate actions during attacks.
- Carson claimed that the Holocaust would not have happened if the German people had been armed

Criminal Sentencing

Carson has made clear statements voicing support for the following crime control measures:

- Use of unnecessary force by the police can be controlled by equipping police with body cameras (The number Carson quoted was that 85% of police brutality instances can be controlled by using body cameras.) he also said that crime rates also drop if the police are wearing body cameras.

- Addressing concerns that the youth seems to be turning to crime in high numbers, he said that there is a need to focus on building inner city resources, which will give the young people and alternative to choosing a life of crime.

- He supports helmet laws and says that motorcyclists have long neglected their safety and that people who fail to comply with safety laws are a burden on the healthcare system.

- Regarding prisons, he has expressed a somewhat unusual view that federal prisons are too comfortable for the prisoner's good and that the environment might be actually causing some prisoners to prefer prison over rehabilitation.

- Regarding people who are convicted of health care fraud, Carson supports imprisonment of at least 10 years and a forfeiture of the individual's personal possessions.

Death Penalty

Carson advocates that the decision about capital punishment should be made on a state-by-state basis. He believes the people of the area should have the final say in this matter. [11] He does not express an outright opposition to the death penalty nor opposes it from any moral/legal standpoint.

War on Drugs

As far as the War on Drugs is concerned, Carson wishes to, in his words, "intensify" it. [12] The War on Drugs has proved to be an unsuccessful policy that has been pursued none the less.

He claims that the government is doing little to control the inflow of drugs from Mexico and he wants to create a double border fence to remedy this.

Many federal agencies are tasked with drugs flowing in from Mexico; billions are spent in these efforts but have been futile. Absolute control remains but a distant dream.

Marijuana Legalization

Carson holds the position supported by majority of the American people and most of the elected officials. He completely opposed to marijuana legalization, he does not believe any good can come out of it, though he does concede that in some compassionate cases,[13] it has proven beneficial.

He considers marijuana a gateway drug and claims that it is not something that we need as a society, according to him it is another step to becoming a hedonistic society. He considers that marijuana legalization will remove the barriers to wide-spread hedonistic activities.

He is also of the opinion that the mainstream media does not openly discuss this issue.

Net Neutrality

Carson does not seem to have the necessary technical knowledge to comment on this issue; in a recent interview his response to the net neutrality issue was not very informative or clear.

He suggested that the principle of having an open internet will lead to increased secrecy and a reduction in privacy. He also claimed that the government was trying to impose an added layer of control through net neutrality.

Voter Registration

Voting rights activists say that voter identification laws and other voter suppression laws have been called racist, Carson disagrees with this view. He said that it is necessary that voting should be done only by appropriate people; he claims that every country in the world has a set of official requirements for voters and that it prevent non-citizens from casting votes.

2. Economic

Corporate Regulation

America has the second highest corporate tax rate in the world, Carson wants to change that. He believes that this is the reason why the national debt is high.

He says that the government is being greedy and is therefore causing companies to other countries. He claims that a low proportional tax rate should be applied to corporate entities.

Carson wishes to slash the U.S. corporate tax rates and create a tax haven [14] for people; he believes it will lead to the creation of an opportunity haven.

He proposes that the rate be between 15%-20%. He plans on giving a 6 month tax-holiday to corporations, this would mean that corporations who hold money overseas would pay 0% tax for half of the year [15] in they invest 10% towards job creation in the US.[16]

Mortgage Crisis

Carson is of the view that the cause of the housing crisis is the deregulation of the financial markets. This view is in stark conflict to the facts that have been made clear so far, the over-regulation of the housing market is what caused the real estate and stock market to collapse.

The rampant and irresponsible lending under the Community Reinvestment Act and the questionable conduct of Fannie Mae worked together to create a perfect storm that led markets to fall.

Budget Deficit

Ben Carson has adopted the old Republican strategy of

campaigning on the platform that centers on efforts to balance the national budget. The current US debt is at $18 trillion and Carson puts the blame for this deficit squarely on the shoulders of Washington and the policies of the past 8 years.

He has said time and again that this debt will cripple future generations with a large burden and the government needs to fix this.

In a speech during his campaign announcement, he claimed that it would take more than 5000 years to pay back the debt if the government made payments of $10 million per day. This staggering amount is probably not far off from the truth.

Carson has stated one major goal: A balanced budget every year [17]

This goal is too broad and requires a lot of detail to be considered a plan. However Carson does not offer many details, he has not defined how he will bring this about, what costs he will cut, how revenues will be grown, what he plans to do with entitlement programs, [18]this is a definite lack he needs to address. The US budget deficit has grown mostly due to increased spending on healthcare and retirement; this is according to a report [19] by the Congressional Budget Office.

Most economists agree that the candidates need to present details about their economic policies or at least flesh out their ideas so the public can get an understanding of what the candidate will actually do, but Carson has not delivered so far, he says that there the priority is to fix the economy before addressing these issues. [20]

Environment vs. Economy

He takes a standard Republican view on this issue, he advocates tapping America's oil reserves in order to end the heavy dependence on foreign oil. But also realizes the importance of clean energy and plans to offer appropriate incentives to make sure investment and research in clean energy solutions is realized.

Off-shore drilling, fracking and expansion of fossil fuels will obviously harm the environment but Carson says that conservation of natural beauty is important but maintaining a powerful position in the global geo-political arena and a high economic growth rate should be given a higher priority.

He does have high support for renewable energy resources; he aims to bring about changes in the energy sector and wants to meet more than 50% of the power demand by 2030 using renewable resources.

Taxation System and Tax Reform

His taxation system is based on tithing, which involves paying one-tenth part of income as tax. Carson is a strong advocate of a flat-tax rate; this would mean that all Americans pay the same rate instead of the graduated scale that is in place now.

He believes that the decision mirrors the Christian god's view of fairness.[21] He has suggested a 10% flat tax rate for every ones, just like the Bible proposes that followers give 10% of their income to the church.

He believes that lower tax rates would help the economy

grow and would eventually generate more revenue. Another stance he has taken is to call for the elimination of the Internal Revenue Service (IRS). His proposed flat tax-rate system would mean a tax increase for millions of Americans.

He plans to reveal his detailed tax plan in the next couple of weeks. Experts agree that candidates have historically indulged in a few overs-simplifications when it comes to understanding the relationship between economic growth and tax cuts.

Oil Drilling

Carson wants America to achieve petroleum independence; he plans on completely eliminating foreign oil imports within the next ten years. This will cripple the economic base of the foreign oil-exporting nations, which he claims are supporting terrorist activities from their oil wealth.

He also wants to expand off-shore drilling and tap natural resources that are available closer at home. He wants to start widespread drilling into the areas under Dakota, Montana, and Alaska and explore off-shore oil reserves.

Climate Change

The candidate is not fully convinced when it comes to considering global warming a threat. He says that the periods of global cooling and warming have been happening for a long time and that the debate on whether humans have caused global warming is irrelevant.

Carson claims that the government is using climate change as an excuse to stagger development of natural God-given resources; he believes it is necessary to preserve the Earth but does not believe that the curtailment of development will help.

He says that government efforts to control greenhouse gas emissions will not help us in the long run.

Renewable Energy

According to Carson, energy can play a role in helping us achieve peace in the world. Carson claims that we should expand our energy resources and put aside fears of an ice age. He also claims in an article written for the Washington Times newspaper that expanding our energy resources serves the purpose of peace.

He wants the EPA (Environmental Protection Agency) to stop making regulations that stifle energy production. [22] Instead the EPA should bring about innovative ways to produce and export green energy to other countries; this will help fortify America's position on the global geo-political stage.

3. Social

Education

Ben Carson is a strong advocate of education and believes in the uplifting power of education. He has been active in the community and has setup a scholarship fund for students who have the grades and the talent cannot afford to go to good colleges. His core beliefs about education management are centered on getting local communities involved.

According to the official campaign website, he wants to give control of education and management of curriculum to local governing levels and make the federal bureaucracy out of the equation. [23]

Common Core

He also wishes to overturn Common Core, the set of academic standards applicable to mathematics and English. Ben Carson wants to put the decision making power in the hands of the parents, teachers and principals and make sure that no "faceless federal bureaucrats" dictate the policies and management of schools.

Public Schools

Mr. Carson wants to revamp the American education system. According to his opinion the system was both efficient and effective in the past than it is now. He claims that America used to have the best education system in the world, but now has ended up in a position where it is the best at creating a propaganda system.

A dramatic change is needed in order to restore the education system to a level where American students can compete with the world.

Views on Homeschooling

He advocates school choice and does not believe in a one-fit solution. He wants people to have the flexibility to decide between what type of schooling they want for their children. He offered the following observations when it comes to school choice:

"Homeschoolers do the best, private schoolers next best, charter schooler's next best, and public schooler's worst. So that's why we need school choice."

Gay Rights and Same-Sex Marriage

Carson has claimed that homosexuality is a choice that people make and he holds this belief "absolutely". [24] He said that prison life serves as proof of this assertion, according to Carson, people go into prison while they are straight and when released they identify as gay.

However the American Psychological Association reveals that scientists cannot definitively say [25] how an individual's sexual orientation develops.

Ben Carson strongly opposes same-sex marriages and holds the view that marriage is between a man and a woman. He " strongly disagreed" with the Supreme Court's decision to allow same-sex marriages, however he respects the decision because it is not the law of the land.[26] (His actual quote was,

"While I strongly disagree with the Supreme Court's decision, their ruling is now the law of the land.")

He claims that marriage is a religious service and not a government for that can be changed. But he supports some sort of civil union that recognizes the right of two adults to retain the benefits traditionally restricted to spouses, such as hospital visitation rights, property rights, etc.

4. National Security and International Policy

Carson has accepted the fact that he is something akin to a novice when it comes to matters of foreign affairs. He stated that he was in the process of acquiring detailed information and was working on developing a thorough understanding of how the foreign policy affects the nation and its interests abroad.

A broad view gleaned from Carson's statements which he made during the campaign and in writings include:

- America needs to clarify its goals when it comes to dealing with the Middle East and the rest of the world.

- Foreign policy matters should not be affected by partisan issues, the country's best interests are above political motives.

- He believes there is a large ethical void in leadership that needs to be filled by America

- He compares America's foreign policy to a rudderless ship, a policy that is proactive but not reactive.

Policy on Terrorism

Carson has expressed a strong view as have other GOP candidates. He says that the US should utilize every means possible to exterminate militant groups such as ISIS. Carson wants to root out terrorism and also focus on Shiite (A major Islamic sect) terrorist groups not just Sunni ones.

Islamic State (ISIS)

The looming threat of ISIL and how the potential presidential candidates will deal with it is a hot button topic ever since the attacks in Paris. ISIS/ISIL claimed responsibility for the attacks and has threatened further attacks, this time on American soil.

Ben Carson has taken a toughest stance and plans to use every option to eliminate these terrorist groups. He plans to work with allies and control the threat using every resource available.[27] But he did not elaborate on what those resources were other than saying that it would be economic and military and in his words "things-that-they-don't-know-about resources."

His stance can be summed up as:

- Remove restrictions on the military and allow them to completely destroy ISIS

- Moderate Muslims have been too quite in this matter, they should condemn the radical elements in their religion

9/11

Carson criticizes the government's response to the 9/11 attacks and says that it cost the American people way too much, both in terms of financial costs and human lives. He believes a better response would have been to

In response to a hypothetical question posed to him, he said that if he had been President during the 9/11 attacks, he would have reacted very differently. Instead of invading Afghanistan, he would have put all his focus towards achieving energy independence.

Another time Carson made the faux pas of comparing the 9/11 attacks with ObamaCare, he called the healthcare reform plan created by the Obama administration as something worse than 9/11.

Iraq War

Carson says that he was not in favor of the Iraq war; he said that had he been in charge, he would not have given the go-ahead for the invasion. He further said that it was a sign of failure as America has not been able to secure the country, which mars the victory claims.

Carson claims that the Bush administration went into the war without knowing what they were getting into. He feels that the government did not pay due attention to the complex history and political factors that were at play on the ground in Iraq.

This is the most common position taken by the candidates, even Jeb Bush said that he would not have gone into Iraq.

Israel/Palestine

Carson is sympathetic towards the cause of the Israelis; he holds the opposite view of the Obama administration as far as the Israeli settlement movement is concerned. He has suggested that if the Palestinian people want a separate state that the neighboring states such as Egypt should provide the required land.

He has been critical of the current administration's stance on the situation and has accused them of not doing enough to support our Israeli allies. [28]

Defense Spending

Carson has expressed the desire to cut federal spending but the defense budget will not be cut. He has called defense cut an "idiotic" proposal. [29] Decisions regarding military funding should focus on what the military leaders want.

He favors removing the ban that has stopped soldiers on military installments from carrying arms. [30]

CHAPTER 8: HILLARY CLINTON: A LIBERAL STANCE ON MAJOR ISSUES

Abortion

Strongly favors abortion and believes it should be a woman's right to have access to abortion without facing any restrictions. Has a pro-choice position and wants to ensure that everyone has access to contraceptives. [31]

Clinton advocates that the focus should be placed on preventing unwanted pregnancies in the first place by providing proper health education, contraceptives and emergency contraceptives. She wants to make sure that abortion is legal but rare and if needed is absolutely safe for the women.

She is also against declaring an unborn child as eligible for the State Children's Health Insurance Program (SCHIP). Further, minors should be able to cross state borders if they want to access to abortion facilities and clinics/hospitals should not be under the obligation to inform the parents of minors who get abortions.

She wants to lift the ban on stem cell research, Clinton says that these research avenues can help cure or treat potentially life-threatening diseases, and she wishes to expand embryonic stem cell research.

Bills sponsored in this regard:

- Provision of emergency contraception for victims of rape

- Easy provision of contraceptives to low-income women

Minorities and Women Rights

Clinton has a pro-affirmative action stance. She takes the following positions when it comes to equal rights for women and minorities:

Advocates inducting more women and minorities in the workforce. Believes that this should be made a legal requirement.

Wants to reinforce equal-pay and anti-discrimination requirements

Everyone should be economically empowered

She has said that some world leaders and rulers are still clinging to their orthodox and misogynistic views. Clinton says that the world has a long way to go when it comes to achieving true equality.

Bills sponsored in this regard:

- Bill which offered protection against pay discrimination based on gender

- A bill which supported the role of women in armed forces

Marriage and Marriage Equality:

Strong supporter of same-sex marriage, Clinton says that the Defense of Marriage Act (DOMA) has held the country back from a more perfect union. She is also against the Federal Marriage Amendment and calls it a terrible step backwards.

Specific stance on gay marriage and gay rights:

- Clinton supports gay marriage, from both a personal standpoint and legal one.

- Gay couples deserve to get domestic partnership benefits

- Military service should not focus on a person's sexual orientation instead the conduct and performance should be paramount.

- Hate crimes should carry stricter criminal penalties and sexual orientation should be included in the definition of hate crimes

Separation of State and Church

Strong proponent of the separation of church and state.

According to Clinton, religion does not belong in the public sphere. She thinks that the Bible should be taught as a piece of history and literature in public schools rather than a source of scientific knowledge or moral principles.

She believes that the government should create partnerships with the faith-based communities in empowerment zones. She says that good education should also focus on teaching empathy and self-discipline.

Clinton believes that while students can be allowed to pray in schools, no school should provide religious instruction.

Protecting the Environment

Clinton is supportive of environmental regulations. She disagrees with the view that Environmental Protection Agency (EPA) regulations are too strict. The specific measures supported by her during her political career are:

Voter Rights

Hillary Clinton has been a tough critic of Voter Registration laws, she says that it they restrict voting rights and discourages young people from participating. Being an avid supporter of having youth more involved in democratic processes she voiced her criticisms vehemently when voter registration laws expanded. The criticism has a valid point in one aspect, these stringent laws reduce voter turnout

Domestic Concerns

Criminal Justice System

Clinton wants to reform the current criminal justice system, which she says is out of balance. The major issues she has highlighted during her campaign are:

- High incarceration rate and high prison population

- The need to recognize that race is a factor when it comes to reforming criminal systems. The patterns of behavior that show this troubling side are obvious in some cases. Clinton has said that "systemic inequities" persist in America's justice system.

Proposed Solutions and Measures:

1. Change the approach to imprisonment and punishment to end mass incarceration

2. Reform the mandatory minimum sentence for non-violent and low-level offenses.

3. She has called for an end to private prisons

4. Implement smart measures and use technology solutions, such as equipping police with body cameras to fight crime and help regain trust of communities

5. The American people need to come to terms and address the harsh realities of race and justice. It is folly to ignore the role that race plays in America, the quicker we accept this the easier our path to true tolerance will become.

6. Help American families across the board, particularly the middle classes to get more economic opportunities and better education so that communities can help themselves.

Gun Control

Clinton strongly disagrees with absolute rights to gun ownership. She says that a background check system should be in place and that dangerous assault weapons and guns in general do not belong in the streets.in order to prevent gun related crimes.

She says that proper gun control measures help protect our children and families. Clinton supports the following measures:

- All handgun sales should be properly registered and licensed
- Increase inspection rules and crack down on gun stores which knowingly sell weapons to criminal elements
- Straw purchasing should be made a federal crime
- Address and close loopholes that enable people with serious mental illnesses to purchase and possess guns
- Military-grade weapons should be kept off the urban and rural streets

- Lawsuits against gun manufacturer should not be banned
- The option for smart guns (which can distinguish between authorized and unauthorized users) should be explored

Healthcare and Reform

Hillary favors expanding ObamaCare, she has previously stated that universal healthcare is core democratic principle. She wants to lower healthcare cost and extend coverage to every individual. The American Public Health Association has voted her views and voting record as 100% pro-public health.

She promises to establish universal health coverage by the end of her second term (if elected). Clinton has called for developing a uniquely American solution for healthcare.

School Vouchers

Clinton has shown strong leanings towards a pro-public school stance in her voting records so far,

Hillary does not support school vouchers; she gives the following reasons for her stance:

- School vouchers are un-constitutional but charter schools are acceptable
- Vouchers tend to become a financial drain on public schools and divert much-needed resources away from where they are needed the most i-e, public schools.

- Implementing them is a major problem because a lot of people would opt for getting school vouchers for schools that teach values that are un-American

Clintons wants smaller classes to eliminate the need for private tutors. Funds should be provided for student testing instead of private tutors.

Early Childhood Education

Hillary has worked towards the goal of providing high-quality pre-kindergarten education to all children. She believes that every child has the right to opportunities that enable them to live up to their full potential.

Lack of proper language development leads to inequalities in vocabulary levels and communication skills. Early childhood education should be funded by government to ensure that children from low-income families and non-English backgrounds close the vocabulary gap.

Early Head Start and Early Head Start–Child Care are two programs that provide education and full-day care for families; they are tailored to serve low-income families. Hillary Clinton wants to double the investment in these two important programs.

Learning starts at an early age, and statistics have shown that if children get quality education early on, their future opportunities increase drastically.

No Child Left Behind Act

A staunch proponent of the No Child Left behind Act, Hillary has plans to provide every American child access to quality education, regardless of race or income level.

She has tried to raise academic standards and supports increasing teacher's salaries. Supporting educators is an important part of this struggle and Hillary plans to take a multi-faceted approach.

Green Energy Alternatives

Clinton strongly favors clean energy initiatives. She has declared a goal of shifting a quarter of American energy production methods to greener alternatives.

The major points of concern on the energy agenda are:

- Plan on reducing fossil fuel usage by 40% by 2025

- Global warming should be factored in to the projects being planned at the federal level

- Oil and gas exploration subsidies currently in place should be removed

- EPA should be funded properly

- Global warming is a natural phenomenon but has been exacerbated by humans

- Supports American energy independence

- Wants to ratify the Kyoto Protocol

- Plans on improving mass transit and lowering the number of fossil-fueled vehicles on the roads, replacing them with hydrogen-powered or electric cars

Drug and Marijuana Legalization

Clinton does not take an extreme stance on this issue, she said that she supports marijuana use if it is for medicinal purposes but wants to adopt a wait-and-see approach when it comes to legalizing recreational use of marijuana.

Clinton want sot see how things turn out in the states that have legalized marijuana, the studies and reports coming out in the near future will elucidate whether the legalization had any positive or negative effects. Clinton considers states the laboratories of democracy, and she says that they can make their own decision when it comes to the legal status of marijuana.

Clinton wants to solve the substance abuse problem in America. Substance abuse is common in all social classes of society. Clinton says that America's small towns as well as major cities are affected by this problem.

Drug abuse causes major losses to the economy as well as people's personal lives. Clinton plans to take the following initiatives to combat the alcohol addiction and rampant drug issues:

- Implement effective prevention programs

- Focus on rehabilitating addicts through proper treatment and recovery
- Provide better control over prescriptions for controlled substances
- Choose better reform programs for criminals involved in drug abuse, shift focus towards treatment instead of imprisonment
- Collaborate with states to allow local leaders develop drug control programs tailored exclusively to community requirements.

Higher Education Reform

Clinton has released a broad and very ambitious plan to reform higher education and help students fund their college fees, the plan has been termed the *'New College Compact Plan'* and includes details about how the presidential hopeful wants to change the face of higher education in the US.

It calls on the federal and state governments, colleges and universities to play their part in easing student loan burdens and enhance college learning.

New College Compact Plan [32]

- The plan will be fully paid for by the government, it will cost about $350 billion over a period of 10 years. [33]
- Imposition of additional regulations on for-profit education
- Significant cut in loan interest rates for future undergraduates
- Provides the ability to refinance previous loans at current rates

- Colleges and universities will have to account for and control costs so that tuition fees remain at an affordable level
- Community college students will be able to get tuition at no cost

Economic Issues

Clinton wants to create a full employment economy which will help create jobs, increase healthy competition among businesses and also result in higher incomes.

The major steps that she will probably support include, raising minimum wage to $15 an hour [34], fixing corporate taxing loopholes and reducing taxes on the middle class. She wants to boost investments in infrastructure, green energy and scientific research.

Clinton plans the following major changes:

- Increase government investment in scientific research.
- Creation of an infrastructure banks that will leverage private and public funds and invest them in projects.
- Increase participation of women and minorities in the labor force
- Encourage companies to focus on long term growth
- Increase accountability of Wall Street, Clinton plans to strengthen financial reforms put in place after the last financial crisis.

Taxation System

- Clinton wants to lower the tax burden on middle class families
- A tax cut of $2500/ student is planned for college students
- Businesses that share profits with the employees will be given tax cuts
- Invest in making small businesses easy to start and run
- Reform the taxation system to ensure that the wealthiest Americans pay their fair share
- Change capital gains tax so that job creators are rewarded

Immigration Policies

Clinton wants to create a fair and just immigration system in the US. The current system needs to change by putting families first and become more humane when it comes to dealing with immigrant families.

The measures proposed by Hillary are broadly outlined below:

- Establish a system that enables deserving immigrants to get a chance at full and equal citizenship [35]
- Reform current immigration legislation
- Continue supporting Obama's Deferred Action for Childhood Arrivals (DACA) and Deferred Action for Parents of Americans (DAPA) executive actions

- Make it a priority to protect immigrant families and enable them easy access to systems that will help them plead their case
- Clinton plans to end family detention for people arriving at the US borders and also close the private immigrant detention centers.
- Expand healthcare coverage to immigrant families

Social Security

Social security programs enable American citizens to retire with dignity. Clinton plans to expand and strengthen social security programs and has declared the following agenda if elected:

- Expand social security to widows and people who take time off from work to look after their children or a sick family member.
- Strengthen the program by asking the wealthy to increase their contributions (via taxes)
- Clinton opposes the reduction of annual adjustments to cost-of-living
- Oppose any efforts to raise the retirement age
- Stop privatization of senior's retirement security

Medicare

The Medicare program offers coverage to over 50 million American people. In her role as Senator, Clinton has backed bills that helped reduce the cost of pharmaceutical drugs for seniors. She plans to enact the following measures when in come to the Medicare program:

- Oppose the repealing or dismantling of the Affordable Care Act, this act provides benefits to millions of seniors.
- Fight Republican efforts to privatize Medicare
- Make drugs and life-saving medicines more affordable for common seniors and other Americans
- Reform the delivery systems of Medicare and improve the value and quality of care that senior citizens are entitled to under this program

Foreign Policy and National Security

When it comes to foreign policy and diplomacy, Clinton believes the country should use a vigorous and bipartisan diplomacy. According to Clinton, America needs to strengthen its alliances with Middle East, Asia and Europe. America's alliance with Israel is important and has been historically strong, Clinton promises to further strengthen this partnership.

China

Clinton has travelled to China frequently and has a firm grasp on the leadership and the country's issues. She acknowledges that the US-China relationships is full of challenges and the complexities are such that both the countries cannot categorize one another as a rival or friend.

- She believes that the following issues are important and both countries need to work on them together:

- Clinton wants China to play a role in North Korean diplomacy efforts
- The US should consider China as a part of a broader Asia-Pacific strategy
- Clinton wants to secure open access to the South China Sea
- The US needs to establish a coherent approach towards diplomatic efforts in China.
- China is a powerful nation and Clinton wants to become a responsible stakeholder and address issues of human rights, solve territorial disputes and take an active role in managing climate change

The Middle East

There are enormous challenges that need to be tackled in a smart and responsible manner. Clinton has the major points on her agenda:

- Iran should not be allowed to acquire a nuclear weapon
- The terrorist group ISIS poses a serious threat to the American people and the allies of US. The strategy to defeat them must contain plans to stabilize the region and not involve the US troops in another hopeless cat-and-mouse game such as Afghanistan.
- Empower American allies in the Middle East so they are capable of defeating terrorism and the fundamentalist ideologies on their own.
- The US needs to help bring stability to Libya and Yemen

Foreign Trade

Clinton is a believer in free people and also free markets. If elected she plans to invest in the Latin American region, Africa as well as Asia. She is also a chief advocate for the Trans-Pacific Partnership (TPP)

Internationalism vs. Isolationism

Clinton has said that America has forgotten the internationalist outlook that has long served the country the best. The political right has seen a shift from this to an attitude of protectionism, and in conjunction have reverted to an isolationist thinking.

Globalization should be embraced with American pre-eminence. A strong global leadership involves having a technologically superior defense instead the US has relied on defense strategies left over from the Cold War era, these need to be revamped and modernized. [36]

America's Role in the Global Arena

Clinton's philosophy centers on building a strong American leadership in the world. [37] The Americans need to lead with a clear purpose in mind and must prove to be principled leaders. Clinton wants to strengthen the US position by making the following efforts:

- Establish a stronger economy and help maintain our diplomatic influence
- Secure the homeland and give the people peace of mind against terrorist threats. Clinton wants to increase efforts to nip terrorism in the bud, by targeting recruitment efforts, combating terrorism propaganda and eliminating safe havens.
- Make the American army technologically superior and ensure that the soldiers are the best-trained and best-equipped.
- Focus on a long-term perspective when it comes to leading the world.

CHAPTER 9: DIFFERING OUTLOOKS ON MAJOR ISSUES

I often find having content within a table format is easiest to do comparisons, so here is one for you.

	Issue	Clinton's View	Carson's View
	Military	Decrease military spending, strengthen international organizations such as the UN and NATO	Supports stronger military, against budget cuts, wants to give more decision-making power to the military leaders
	Gun Control	Gun control laws must be stringent and implemented properly	Law abiding people should have unhindered access to guns
	Global Warming	America and the world needs to alter their lifestyle and focus on controlling	Climate change is a natural phenomenon, there is no need to

		the runaway warming	alter habits or consider it a national priority
	Gay Rights	Supports gay marriage personally and as a law of the land	Opposed to gay marriage on religious grounds but supports civil unions
	Minimum Wage	The working poor deserve to get a living wage	Against the issue. Hold the view that increasing minimum wage drives up joblessness
	Death Penalty	Supports a restricted version of it	Pro. But wants states to decide on legislation
	Taxes and Tax-cuts	Taxes need to go to people who have the most money	Taxes should stay low, advocate of tax cuts
	Government	Government can be big if needed	Remain as small as possible
	Flag Burning	A part of freedom of speech	Should not be allowed
	Illegal Immigration	Wants to give a path to citizenship for current illegals. Deportation of	Put up border walls if needed, create a guest worker program

		criminals.	
	Religion	State and church are separate and should remain so	Christian values are a part of life and should not be suppressed in any way
	Education	Promotes choice among public schools	Parents should decide between public or private
	College	Education from pre-school to college is a right. Make college more affordable and introduce apprenticeships	Schools should pay off the interest rates on college loans.
	Abortion	Women have the right to choose. Plans to bring down rates by proper sex education, offering better adoption and fostering care. Respect Roe v. Wade.	Entirely pro-life. Wants to ban abortions in cases where 20 weeks have passed since fertilization

CHAPTER 10: CONCLUSION

Clinton and Carson are tough players and have been distinguished in their respective field, if they both manage to secure the nomination from their parties, then the election next year will prove to be one of the most interesting ones in the past decades. They differ widely when it comes to important matters.

Whoever happens to secure the presidency, it will be a historical moment, if Clinton wins then she will be the first female President of the United States, landmark achievement. If Carson manages to get elected then the world will see the first US President that has not previously held any elected office.

These candidates present their views and plans in details, it is up to the public to carefully analyze these positons and make the right decision when they head to the polls next year. The campaigns are far from over, things will pick up pace as the election nears, even if these two do not manage to secure the nomination, they will definitely play a role in their respective parties.

Carson has managed to wow the conservatives and the

staunch Republicans, he has garnered massive support in a very short time. This is obviously in contrast to Clinton who works at a slow pace, perfecting every move.

The two have vastly differing approach to the politics and the Presidential office, a clear understanding of their motives and potential capabilities will help the average voter make the best decision. There are other candidates also vying for the nomination, only time will tell if they manage to secure it. The coming year will prove to be a major game changer, the new President will face police challenges both inside America and on a global scale. Whoever the American people choose will have the difficult task of dealing with challenges such as the threat of terrorism, economic slowdowns, international conflicts that threaten to spill over into neighboring nations, nuclear proliferation, and a myriad of tasks that will demand working with allies and reluctant partners in the world.

The American Presidency is called the hardest job in the world, any role which involves a lot of power comes more responsibility than the person bargained for, most of these candidates have proved their mettle and some have yet to shine.

ABOUT THE AUTHOR

Michael Joshua got his undergraduate degree in Finance and works full time at a large bank as a Financial Analyst. He has great knowledge in Business & Money, along with politics and technology.

Goodreads:

https://www.goodreads.com/user/show/46377085-michael-joshua

Twitter:

https://twitter.com/mjoshua_author

Footnotes

1. http://www.biography.com/people/ben-carson-475422#beginning-surgical-career
2. http://thehill.com/blogs/ballot-box/gop-primaries/259438-carson-rebukes-media-for-witch-hunt
3. http://edition.cnn.com/2015/11/05/politics/ben-carson-2016-childhood-violence/
4. http://www.wsj.com/articles/ben-carsons-past-faces-deeper-questions-1446861864
5. http://www.esquire.com/news-politics/politics/news/a39579/ben-carson-debunked-west-point/
6. http://www.politico.com/story/2015/11/ben-carson-west-point-215598
7. http://www.brookings.edu/blogs/fixgov/posts/2015/11/10-republican-debate-carson-caricature-candidate-hudak
8. http://www.biography.com/people/hillary-clinton-9251306#early-years
9. https://www.whitehouse.gov/1600/first-ladies/hillaryclinton
10. http://www.refinery29.com/2015/10/95494/ben-carson-gun-violence-offensive-comments
11. http://www.chicagotribune.com/news/opinion/commentary/ct-ben-carson-death-penalty-lubet-perspec-1113-20151112-story.html
12. http://www.theatlantic.com/politics/archive/2015/10/ben-carson-intensify-the-war-on-drugs-and-keep-marijuana-illegal/411868/
13. http://www.theatlantic.com/politics/archive/2015/10/ben-carson-intensify-the-war-on-drugs-and-keep-marijuana-illegal/411868/
14. http://www.huffingtonpost.com/entry/ben-carson-tax-policy_5616a91be4b0e66ad4c6d9a0

15. http://www.cnbc.com/2015/10/07/dr-ben-carson-would-declare-a-6-month-tax-hiatus-for-profits-held-overseas.html

16. http://www.taxjusticeblog.org/archive/2015/09/ben_carsons_10_percent_flat_ta.php

17. http://money.cnn.com/2015/09/10/news/economy/ben-carson-economic-policy/

18. http://money.cnn.com/2015/09/10/news/economy/ben-carson-economic-policy/

19. https://www.cbo.gov/sites/default/files/114th-congress-2015-2016/reports/50724-BudEconOutlook.pdf

20. http://www.npr.org/sections/itsallpolitics/2015/10/30/452905475/fact-check-do-tax-cuts-grow-the-economy

21. http://money.cnn.com/2015/08/07/news/economy/republican-debate-economic-ideas/?iid=EL

22. http://www.nytimes.com/2015/05/04/us/politics/ben-carson-on-the-issues.html

23. https://www.bencarson.com/issues/education/

24. http://www.huffingtonpost.com/2015/03/04/ben-carson-gay-prison_n_6799160.html

25. http://www.apa.org/topics/lgbt/orientation.aspx

26. http://talkingpointsmemo.com/livewire/ben-carson-gay-marriage-decision

27. http://www.nbcnews.com/storyline/isis-terror/dr-ben-carson-use-every-means-possible-fight-terror-n315176

28. http://www.nytimes.com/2015/05/04/us/politics/ben-carson-on-the-issues.html

29. http://www.washingtonexaminer.com/ben-carson-cutting-defense-spending-is-idiotic/article/2564972

30. http://www.2016committee.org/issues#military

31. http://www.ontheissues.org/Hillary_Clinton.htm

32. https://www.hillaryclinton.com/p/briefing/factsheets/2015/08/10/college-compact/

33. http://edition.cnn.com/2015/08/10/politics/hillary-clinton-college-affordability/

34. http://useconomy.about.com/od/fiscalpolicy/p/Hillary_Economy.htm
35. http://abcnews.go.com/Politics/hillary-clinton-reveals-plans-immigration-reform/story?id=30812123
36. http://www.politico.com/blogs/ben-smith/2009/07/clintons-internationalism-019876
37. http://carnegieendowment.org/2015/10/23/clinton-transcends-committee-cynicism/ik8e